The Collaborative Podcast Series; Book 1

The Foundations for Collaboration

By David B. Savage

Table of Contents

Foreword 1

Define your personal values as a successful collaborative
leader.. 11

Chapter 1 Finding Your Truth..13

Chapter 2 10 Essential Steps to Collaboration 19

Chapter 3 Great Leaders Know That They Don't Know.... 25

Chapter 4 Global Book Release Celebration........................31

Chapter 5 EGOS 37

Chapter 6 How Collaborative is my organization?............ 43

Chapter 7 Collaboration is the Way; Shared Value is the
Destination.. 49

Chapter 8 Building Your Collaborative Culture 55

Guests on the Collaborative Podcast Series

In order of appearance on the podcasts, I thank these friends, mentors and collaborative leaders;

Chuck Rose, Denise Chartrand, Kathy Porter, Duncan Autrey, Jeanne McPherson, Allan Davis, Patricia Morgan, Don Loney, David Gouthro, Kenneth Cloke, Cheryl Cardinal, Ryan Robb, Esther Bleuel, Jeffrey Cohen, Joan Goldsmith, Amy Fox, Richard Schultz, Laura Hummelle, Colin Campbell, Donna Hastings, Rob McKay, Art Korpach, Tara Russell, Linda Matthie, Viki Winterton, Stephen Smith, Dee Ann Turner, Doreen Liberto, Dana Meise, Teresa de Grosbois, David Milia, Don Simmons, Bruce McIntyre, James Armstrong, Michael Hill, Johanne Lavoie, Atul Tandon, Prabha Sankaranarayan, Bob Anderson, Dan Savage, Sarah Daitch, India Sherri, Kevin Brown, David Milia, AnnaMarie McHargue, Bob Acton, David Mitchell, Tristen Chernove, Martin Parnell, Mike Thompson, Stephen Hobbs, Julie Murray, Doreen Liberto, Chuck Rose, Elisabeth Delaygue Bevan, Florian Wackermann, Lance Kadatz, Cliff Wiebe, Amy Schabacker Dufrane, Japman Bajaj, Kate McKenzie, Shawn Anderson, Martin Parnell, Jim Gibson, Jeffrey Cohen, Barry Wilson, Doreen Liberto, Jeffrey Cohen, Deva Premal and Miten, Klara Fenlof, Robert Stewart, Sara Amos and Quinn Amos, Kenneth Cloke, and Duncan Autrey.

This is Break Through To Yes: The Collaborative Podcast Series by David B. Savage

Book 1: The Foundations for Collaboration
includes eight 15-minute podcasts originally aired on the Tenacious Living Network.

1. Finding Your Truth
2. 10 Essential Steps to Collaboration
3. Great Leaders Know That They Don't Know
4. Global Book Release Celebration
5. EGOS
6. How Collaborative is my organization?
7. Collaboration is the Way; Shared Value is the Destination
8. Building Your Collaborative Culture

Thank you to Tenacious Living Network for originally producing these episodes.

Let's work together better for our shared future.

Imagine the peaks we will reach together.

Collaboration is the path.

Foreword

I've been asked many times: why have I done this podcast series? Why have I written Break Through to Yes: Unlocking the Possible within a Culture of Collaboration? Why is this so important? Why did I lead the group that created the book Let's Talk, a handbook for dispute resolution between companies in Company Dispute Resolution?

I'll tell you why. We need it. I need it. Our future needs it. Business is forced into silos and has to give up to an open an agile system that better suit today's world and the future. We must create shared value. The cost of command and control leadership are getting higher.

During my 42-year career in the business, I've held titles including director, president, and chief operating officer. I have seen many and repeated failures, sometimes with the cost of billions. These affect organizations and their capital projects and operations. When a company starts making mistakes, tries to force its agenda on others, or is in conflict with its own stakeholders, the consequences are significant. People revolt and profit margins are destroyed. Projects get delayed in regulatory and community review for extended lengths of time. Employees simply don't give their best because they do not trust the systems they work in especially when they have little influence in the processes or programs in which they are involved.

The cost to organizations can be both internal and external disengagement, rejection by regulatory bodies and governments, rejection by impacted communities, and damage to the environment. Add to that a wide range of human cause including everything from the oppression, conflict, suicide, marital breakdown and career paralysis to the loss of intelligence and vision of the brightest people in your business, simply because they mentally check out when they come to work.

All this means lost productivity, lost opportunities to grow and prosper, and distracted leaders and workers who no longer feel able to do good work. Leaders and organizations however can gain a strategic advantage by avoiding all of these energy and revenue-zapping negativity simply by working together to build a culture of collaboration.

Collaboration is not an event, it's a culture. It's the way we work together. I am a lifelong student of how to get the right people in the right place with the right information in the right mindset to figure out how to conquer challenges and solve conflicts together.

Collaboration is a new field of study and success. Collaboration must evolve. Let's learn together and make our world, communities and families better. That's my why. What's yours?

This is a quote from an OpEd article By Thomas L. Freidman in the New York Times September 27, 2017;

"When work was predictable and the change rate was relatively constant, preparation for work merely required the codification and transfer of existing knowledge and predetermined skills to create a stable and deployable work force," explains education consultant Heather McGowan. "Now that the velocity of change has accelerated, due to a combination of exponential growth in technology and globalization, learning can no longer be a set dose of education consumed in the first third of one's life." In this age of accelerations, "the new killer skill set is an agile mind-set that values learning over knowing."

Collaboration is a new field of study and success. Collaboration must evolve. Let's learn together and make our world, communities and families better. That's my why. What's yours?

Welcome. I am David B. Savage. This compilation of my podcasts is created to provide you, in one source, the deep look at how we work together and how we can do that better. I offer you this compilation of 41 podcasts for your enjoyment, education, and leadership.

When I started writing my book Break Through to Yes: Unlocking the Possible within a Culture of Collaboration, I realized in 2012 that there were few books on collaboration and none of them were collaborative books. This series of podcasts, 41 podcasts, is not about me. It's about "we". It's about "we" and how to create shared value.

In my books and podcasts, I offer you insights from my 42+ years of business leadership, plus the wisdom from over 175 leaders from eight countries around the world. Yeah, the book and the podcasts have over 175 other voices.

I hope you'll add yours. Email me to share your learning and insights. Let's collaborate. I believe that through leadership, excellence and collaboration, we can make our personal and professional lives far better together.

In this compilation, you will experience many perspectives and dreams. It's divided in four easy to listen to and read books.

I)   Book 1: The Foundations for Collaboration

offers you eight 15-minute podcasts originally aired on the Tenacious Living Network, a quick hit, a series of eight 15-minute podcasts.

II)   Book 2: The Collaborative Guest Podcasts

offers you three podcasts where I had been a guest on Barry Wilson, Bob Acton and Duncan Autrey's podcasts. The subjects are collaboration and negotiation, leadership and cumulative environmental effects on our landscape.

III)   Book 3: The 10 Essential Steps of Collaboration

provides you with 16 podcasts originally aired on Voice America. In addition to the 10 Essential Steps, this Book includes the Next Generation of Leaders and our Shared Future.

IV)   Book 4: Unlocking the Possible with Collaboration

provides you with a further 14 podcasts originally aired on Voice America. These podcasts feature collaboration and Disruptive Technology, Organizational Assessments, Critical Thinking, Sports, Leadership and combating human Sexual trafficking with collaboration.

Plus, there's a bonus in our podcasts. You will hear the beautiful music of Chuck Rose, Deva Premal and Miten, and Led to Sea.

Note; The chapters and books are transcripts from the podcasts. These are not edited and/ or re-written for the Collaborative Podcast Series. These are the brilliant unpolished conversations.

Welcome to our collaborative podcast series. Let's collaborate for a better shared future for our people, planet, and communities. Welcome. Thank you. And let's be better together. Let's Create Shared Value.

In my talks, writing and consulting, I focus on CSV. There is a chapter in Book 1 specifically on Creating Shared Value plus videos on my YouTube Channel. What is CSV? Along with collaboration, critical thinking and leadership, Creating Shared Value is our path to our shared future.

Let's define Creating Shared Value and Critical Thinking.

What is Creating Shared Value?

The Harvard Business Review says it best in the January – February 2011 issue How To Fix Capitalism, Michael E. Porter and Mark R. Kramer write;

"The capitalist system is under siege. In recent years business has been criticized as a major cause of social, environmental, and economic problems. Companies are widely thought to be prospering at the expense of their communities. Trust in business has fallen to new lows, leading government officials to set policies that undermine competitiveness and sap economic growth. Business is caught in a vicious circle.

A big part of the problem lies with companies themselves, which remain trapped in an outdated, narrow approach to value creation. Focused on optimizing short-term financial performance, they overlook the greatest unmet needs in the market as well as broader influences on their long-term success. Why else would companies ignore the well-being of their customers, the depletion of natural resources vital to their businesses, the viability of suppliers, and the economic distress of the communities in which they produce and sell?

It doesn't have to be this way, say Porter, of Harvard Business School, and Kramer, the managing director of the social impact advisory firm FSG. Companies could bring business and society back together if they redefined their purpose as creating "shared value"—generating economic value in a way that also produces value for society by addressing its challenges. A shared value approach reconnects company success with social progress.

Firms can do this in three distinct ways: by reconceiving products and markets, redefining productivity in the value chain, and building supportive industry clusters at the company's locations. A number of companies known for their hard-nosed approach to business—including GE, Wal-Mart, Nestlé, Johnson & Johnson, and Unilever—have already embarked on important initiatives in these areas. Nestlé, for example, redesigned its coffee procurement processes, working intensively with small farmers in impoverished areas who were trapped in a cycle of low productivity, poor quality, and environmental degradation. Nestlé provided advice on farming practices; helped growers secure plant stock, fertilizers, and pesticides; and began directly paying them a premium for better beans. Higher yields and quality increased the growers' incomes, the environmental impact of farms shrank, and Nestlé's reliable supply of good coffee grew significantly. Shared value was created.

Shared value could reshape capitalism and its relationship to society. It could also drive the next wave of innovation and productivity growth in the global economy as it opens managers' eyes to immense human needs that must be met, large new markets to be served, and the internal costs of social deficits—as well as the competitive advantages available from addressing them. But our understanding of shared value is still in its genesis. Attaining it will require managers to develop new skills and knowledge and governments to learn how to regulate in ways that enable shared value, rather than work against it."

What is Critical Thinking?

"Critical thinking is self-guided, self-disciplined thinking which attempts to reason at the highest level of quality in a fair-minded way. People who think critically consistently attempt to live rationally, reasonably, empathically. They are keenly aware of the inherently flawed nature of human thinking when left unchecked. They strive to diminish the power of their egocentric and sociocentric tendencies. They use the intellectual tools that critical thinking offers – concepts and principles that enable them to analyze, assess, and improve thinking. They work diligently to develop the intellectual virtues of intellectual integrity, intellectual humility, intellectual civility, intellectual empathy, intellectual sense of justice and confidence in reason. They realize that no matter how skilled they are as thinkers, they can always improve their reasoning abilities and they will at times fall prey to mistakes in reasoning, human irrationality, prejudices, biases, distortions, uncritically accepted social rules and taboos, self-interest, and vested interest. They strive to improve the world in whatever ways they can and contribute to a more rational, civilized society. At the same time, they recognize the complexities often inherent in doing so. They avoid thinking simplistically about complicated issues and strive to appropriately consider the rights and needs of relevant others. They recognize the complexities in developing as thinkers, and commit themselves to life-long practice toward self-improvement. They embody the Socratic principle: The unexamined life is not worth living, because they realize that many unexamined lives together result in an uncritical, unjust, dangerous world." Linda Elder, September 2007 as reported by the Critical Thinking Community website.

"A well cultivated critical thinker:

- ✓ raises vital questions and problems, formulating them clearly and precisely;
- ✓ gathers and assesses relevant information, using abstract ideas to interpret it effectively comes to well-reasoned conclusions and solutions, testing them against relevant criteria and standards;
- ✓ thinks open-mindedly within alternative systems of thought, recognizing and assessing, as need be, their assumptions, implications, and practical consequences; and
- ✓ communicates effectively with others in figuring out solutions to complex problems.

Critical thinking is, in short, self-directed, self-disciplined, self-monitored, and self-corrective thinking. It presupposes assent to rigorous standards of excellence and mindful command of their use. It entails effective communication and problem-solving abilities and a commitment to overcome our native egocentrism and sociocentrism."

Richard Paul and Linda Elder, The Miniature Guide to Critical Thinking Concepts and Tools, Foundation for Critical Thinking Press, 2008

What is Collaboration?

Here is an except from Break Through To Yes: Unlocking the Possible within a Culture of Collaboration.

"When you Google "collaboration" you get at least 278,000,000 results. [Note if you searched Collaboration on Google in October 2017, you would have received 530,000,000,000 results. This is almost a double in just two years. 530 million results. 187% increase. Will we reach a billion in 2018? There is a significant and growing interest in collaboration.]

Seems there is a lot of interest in learning about collaboration. But what is collaboration represented as?

Merriam Webster defines collaborate as "to work with another person or group in order to achieve or do something." This could be the definition of a meeting or what a football team does. I prefer this definition:

"Collaboration is highly diversified teams working together inside and outside a company with the purpose to create value by improving innovation, customer relationships and efficiency while leveraging technology for effective interactions in the virtual and physical space."

Let's make a joint proclamation that we value collaboration as a powerful way of leading. Collaboration isn't an act, it is the way we lead. To collaborate isn't simply to work together, it is an organizational culture."

And from What Is Collaboration at Work? By Bruce Mayhew, HuffPost July 24, 2014;

"Collaboration is the successful structure of the future - not a single conversation between two employees. A diverse and collaborative culture is a powerful competitive advantage. A well-implemented, trained and supported high-performance team will better align their outcomes around both their objective and company mission.

Tomorrows successful organizations recognize that in today's complex professional environment that collaboration is critical.

Collaborative leaders recognizes there will be challenges and that their greatest responsibility is to guide change and future success by preparing their employees to overcoming these challenges in a respectful and mindful way."

Define your personal values as a successful collaborative leader

Name five values: (for example, integrity, transparency, fairness, innovative, inclusive, curiosity, accountability, intelligence, courageous, perfection, altruism, loyalty, respect, family, humility, truth, determination, independence, ...

1)
2)
3)
4)
5)

How do you choose to lead?

_____
_____
_____

What resources do you need (human, technology, networks, financial, environmental, social)?

_____
_____
_____

What do you choose to let go of to make this so?

_____
_____
_____

What else?

_____
_____
_____
_____

Chapter 1 Finding Your Truth

Welcome to Break Through to Yes with Collaboration, where it's all about working together to build a strong culture of collaboration within organizations. Host David B. Savage, business leader and consultant has over 40 years of experience shaping collaborative cultures. He believes that now is the time to lead more powerfully, consciously and collaboratively in ways that make our world a better place today and in the future. Unlock the possible within a culture of collaboration. Say yes to this opportunity and join a movement of progressive, principled and successful leaders.

Now, here's your host, David B. Savage.

David: Hi. I want to talk and share my passion about collaboration with you. My book is out and you wonder why this podcast, why me, why you. Well, I think you are looking beyond the separation, the misunderstandings. You want to work together better. This is how we choose and this is different than what it's been often times in organizations and business, in families. So why you? Well this podcast I hope will really serve you. It will give you some tools, some techniques, some stories about collaboration. One of the things I did in starting to write Break Through to Yes back in 2012 was the realization that collaboration is so overused and misunderstood.

Why collaborate? Why not do it yourself? The other night, I sat down and gave myself some time just to watch a documentary and a special at a movie. One was the Inner Workings of Donald Trump. The other one was the movie Steve Jobs. What I noticed is both men are very, very successful, very influential, respected by millions and yet to a large extent, they were wanting to be heroes, wanting to be at the top of the pyramid, in charge. They ticked a lot of people off in their journey. So, if you're looking for that style of rock star leadership, this podcast probably isn't the best place for you. If you're looking to move your whole organization together, to build it together, to celebrate together, to succeed in ways that you haven't been able to, you're exactly at the right spot. Welcome. Thanks for spending this short time with me.

So, this podcast, I noticed that in my life, we're all busy, I'm busy, you're busy. Oftentimes, we only can take snippets so we've decided just to do a 15-minute podcast, the whole series. Give you a snippet, give you a thought. The thing that I really want to talk about today is two things, Donald Trump and Steven Jobs and what that culture is and then the more sustainable culture of teamwork, working together better, finding your truth. Not their truth, not what's marketed but your truth. Finding your truth, that's the theme for this podcast.

If you drive to rock star status, drive to I'm in charge and I'm going to condemn the rest of the world or I'm going to condemn the man that founded Apple with me, Wozniak. Yeah, there are plenty of examples of how that can be very successful and I can't discount it. Those two men, Trump and Jobs have been way more successful than David Savage, as or will be. We believe and you're listening to day because you believe that working together is far more challenging and far more rewarding. Part of the rewards is collaborative wisdom, collaborative ways. Collaborative collective intelligence is far smarter, far more inclusive, far more creative than one person at the top trying to do it all. They can't do it all. We see in politics especially the divisiveness, the abuse, the bullying and often times bullies get bullied. Often times we say, "Hmm, why is that person doing that? That's disrespectful."

Finding our truth. Let me tell you an example of finding our truth. An example, over the years I've gathered friends around the world. This particular friend who lives in Boston, she is very passionate about sustainability, environmental protection and she's a great business person. She is somebody I really adore. She was on Facebook I think it was about six, eight months ago, and I saw a post, the post read something like 'BP has spilled Tar Sands oil in the rivers of Chicago. We must stop BP. We must stop Tar Sands. We must save our environment. We must save Chicago.' So, this is a conversation that I think is an example of the separation, division, the things that Donald Trump likes to do and many others. He's emotionally triggered us, emotionally set us up to respond, react, get the reptilian portion of our brain up to trot.

I wrote back to her and said, "Gee, I need some information here. I've Googled BP, oil spill, Tarzan, Chicago and I'm not seeing anything. What do you know that I don't know?" And her response is very quick and clear, "Well, interest group X posted this on Facebook and I wanted to share it. I believe in what they're doing." My response is, "Just like my book, come together, find your truth," and that's the subject to this podcast, find your truth. We have the means that we don't have to check in with social media, check in with Donald Trump, Apple, Ford, Monsanto, Safeway, Whole Foods. Whatever that is, we can find out own truth. It was that there's only six degrees of separation between anyone of us in the world. I think that shrunk in 2016. I believe there's only two degrees of separation.

So, I had to respond to my friend in Boston about "Tar Sands that are "produced by BP and are being spilled in the waters around Chicago". I invited her to a collaboration, an opportunity for us to learn together. I have environmentalist friends. I have a network and a company that works on sustainability for companies. I have friends who work for BP. I have friends who work in the oil sands or the Tar Sands as activists like to call them. I invited her, "Let's get together. A group of perhaps six people. We'll do a Skype or Zoom meeting and we'll have a conversation for 15 to 20 minutes. And let's stop knowing the result in advance, let's stop claiming and judging. Let's actually use this opportunity to Break Through to our truth, Break Through to our yes, Break Through to possibilities. What I want to see is that Skype conversation with Boston, with BP, with environmentalist, with Chicago, with oil women, and others about the Tar Sands. Let's use the first part of that half-hour meeting to say, 'All right. Hello. What are our intentions? How do we engage with trust, inclusion, respect, listening deeply? How do we find out our truth? What are the key issues and interest that we want to Break Through to? Where do we go from here? That is the open space.'" And guess what, we didn't take time to even meet, let alone set that open space up. Too often, we have a "Love Fest for the Self Righteous" This happens in all isolated sides of divisive issues. Where is the collaboration?

I think it would have been brilliant and I think we can get through the lobbying by oil and gas professionals and associations. We can get through the lobbying by environmentalist groups. We can actually Break Through to our own yes. So, I invite you, when your reptilian brain, your amygdala starts to react, you start to get upset, engaged, enraged, start asking, "Is this my truth? What do I need to know? Who are the people that are within two degrees of separation of me that I can connect with?" Who are they? Let's connect with them. Let's find out a shared truth. Let's find out your truth. It doesn't have to be shared, maybe that the wrong word. Share respect, share collaboration, shared questions and let us make up our own minds. There can't be anything more important in this day than making up our own minds. Otherwise, we're led like sheep. Otherwise, we become a reactive as oppose to an intelligent organization. A reactive as oppose to an intelligent leader. A reactive versus an intelligent community.

In my book, Break Through to Yes: Unlocking the

Possible Within a Culture of Collaboration, I provide 10 steps, 10 essential steps to collaboration. Check it out. Hope you buy it. Hope it works for you. More importantly, I hope for intelligent communications, conversations, collectives and I hope we take control of the conversation. Yes, Donald Trump has millions of followers. Hillary Clinton has millions of followers. Their truth isn't my truth. My truth is different. My truth is based on a life, a 40-year career as an environmentalist, as an oil man, as a connector, as a coach, as a speaker, as a writer. What's your truth? Tell us your truth.

So, check it out. Every time you get enraged, engaged consider, "How do I find my truth? Who do I reach out to? What are the key questions here?" Let's get beyond everybody's individual and organizational interest. Come together, there might have bonus in this. Is once you form that collaborative Skype conversation or Zoom or telephone conversation or a campfire, whatever that is, you build new relationships, you're communicating, teaching and learning and connecting most importantly with people that are different than me, different than you. Inclusion, various perspectives, there is the power of collaboration. There is the power of collaboration. There is finding your truth. I talk about my 10 steps. I invite you to consider consciously what your truth is.

One of the things I will tell you is collaboration is the most misunderstood word. Well, sustainability is probably equal to it. Sustainability isn't just about being green, it's being in community, in business. Collaboration is challenging. Few of us do it well. Few of us actual know what it means. In another podcast, I'm going to walk through the 10 steps for you and just for this moment, understand that that ten steps to collaboration. Step six is where we actually get together. Aren't you curious as to what happens on the first five steps? It's like any relationship. It's like making love. It's like community. It's like business. It's like environmental protection and politics. It takes time before you can go where you want to go, get what you want to get. It takes time so please take the time. Be conscious as a collaborator, find what your truth is. And today, I challenge you.

Here's a challenge. When you get engaged, enraged, the hair goes up in the back of your neck, ask, "How do I find my truth? Who could I talk with? How do I connect with them? What are the questions I like to have?" from multiple perspectives, not just one. This is not a coffee shop conversation. This is intentional. And we will change our world together. We will change our world. Thank you.

Chapter 2 10 Essential Steps to Collaboration

David: Greetings. I want to talk to you today about my 10 essential steps to collaboration. This is David B. Savage. So why Break Through to Yes: Unlocking the Possibility Within a Culture of Collaboration? It's because I see so much dysfunction, disvaluing, segregation, separation, judgment. I see so many values stepped on and I see so much value for shareholders destroyed. So, in my book, part of it is about creating this 10-step process. That's what we want to talk about today. I want to help you collaborate and achieve your success. But why this podcast? Well, I'm reaching out to number of ways in the last year, blogs, podcasts, webinars, speaking, workshops, coaching, consulting, any way that I can serve you. Then why a 15-minute podcast? Well, what I've found in our world, we are quite distracted, distractible. Sometimes we can only hold our focus for moments or minutes.

I've been doing hour-long podcasts and the fantastic thing about those ones is I was reaching listeners in 30 different countries around the world. When I looked at my analytics, I noticed most people listen for an average of 24 minutes, so that's great but let's make it consumable in a limited timeframe where you can just check in for 15 minutes and listening to this podcast series. I really hope this serves you or I hope it serves me as well. Mostly, I hope it changes the way we work together, the way we are.

So, the heart of my brand-new book, Break Through to Yes: Unlocking the Possible Within a Culture of Collaboration. There are 10 essential steps today in this podcast. That's what we're going to talk about. Here's a note. Most people when they think about collaboration, they don't know what that is. They think it's getting together. We're going to get together and do something. Not quite sure what that is, what it looks like, who's there, why. Getting together isn't until step six of my 10 Essential Steps. Think about that, be a conscious leader, a conscious in-the-moment collaborator, really be aware. So, if you know that you pay the cost of bad collaborations, bad leadership whether it's your boss, your community, your politicians, whether it's even you. I know at times I do things very badly and I'm always looking to improve.

So, let's walk through the 10 steps as your guide. They're in my book, they're also in my website. Look at those 10 steps, look at all the resources that are there, videos, assessments, blogs. But let's go if you want to avoid the pain of bad collaboration, bad leadership.

Step 1 – Set Intention, declare your honest purpose. So, this is a mindfulness of present scene. What am I really seeking to achieve here? Honestly, what is the outcome? Now, I found if I lock into an outcome, then I lock out other possibility. So often when executives come to me and say, "David, will you work with us on this project or within our organization to develop our culture?" One of the key questions now is how comfortable are you with not knowing the outcome? Few business leaders are, they've got their objective, their goal, their target, their budget but just be aware, your intention is to collaborate in all its beauty, in all its challenges for whatever the collective wisdom bring to the group. It's Break Through to a greater yes.

Step 2 – Be Aware, engage others with an open heart. Often, you'll realize that people in your organization, in your community, your family don't have the same drive, the same motivation, the same interest as you. Often, they're just watching, they're not really engaged. Understand what their alternatives are. Understand what they'd prefer. Are they monitoring and maybe blocking, gathering information or are they fully in.

If they're blocking, that moves us to step 3 –
embrace conflict, seek out those that speak out. So, don't
get sucked in to yes man group think. When people speak
out and push back on me, that's a gift. There's something
very important to them that they think that I'm not
respecting. They give me the opportunity to learn. They
give me an opportunity to include for the greater outcome.
Give them a voice.

Step 4 – Seek Diversity, bring in many perspectives.
Young, old, black white, whatever culture. Bring in the
Serbians. Bring in the Inuit. Bring in the Piikani. Whoever
those people are that will be affected by your collaboration,
bring them in. It's like having a constructive critic. It's like
having somebody that doesn't see the way I see it. What a
gift? Because if you deny them here, they will show up
later and that will not be productive.

Step 5 – Design the Collaboration, imagine success
and create the right container. Who are the right people,
what is the right time, the right place, the right resources,
the right intentions? Even the physical design, architects,
interior designers design spaces based on how do we create
a space that creates innovation, creativity. Think about
going outside. Think about having your collaboration
under a tree, under a thousand-year-old tree, around a
campfire. Think about sitting in that field that's going to
be affected, connecting to the earth. Yeah, it's not that
hard but it's not that common.

Step 6 of my 10 Essential Steps: Come Together.
Yeah, come together, meet, engage with respect and trust.

Step 7 – Listen Deeply, realize what wants to be
heard but it's not spoken. So, in my coaching certification,
we reviewed four levels of listening. First level is listening
to the words of the person in front of you who's saying.
The fourth level is listening to the energy in the room,

reach the energy. Is there something here in this room that isn't being spoken that wants to be spoken?

Step 8 – Collaborate with Vision, tap into the collective wisdom. Yeah, the collective wisdom. This often starts from, where do we want to be together five years from now, ten years from now? What's our future desired state for our organization, four our company, for our community? Whatever that is, what is our future desired state? Based on your values, based on the principles, based on the resources available, the challenges and opportunities in your organizations or community, those need to be understood, explored, and find a vision. Is your vision just a bunch of one offs in whatever comes out for the collective, too bad? Or is it something that you as leader can agree with, the environmentalist, the youth, the chamber of commerce, the politicians? Is it something that you can agree together? This is where we're going, this is where we want to be, and this is how we will all collaborate.

Step 9 - Now lead, now, this comes to the traditional leadership. Often people will collaborate when they don't want to lead. Death by consultation, death by collaboration. No, it's both. The first eight steps, you as leader are holding the space, creating the container, building the power, the culture, the innovation, the creativity, the "but". Even saying that, I can feel it. Now lead. Let's talk about purpose, let's talk about measurables, accountability. Time to step into that leadership role. You are the driver.

Step 10 – Make It So, so positively change the energy and the future together. Continual collaboration, continual evolution, learning together. Continual 10 steps, keep going, keep going, keep going.

So, in this podcast, I hope this has been helpful to you, my 10 Essentials Steps to Collaboration. You can use it in many forms. It is a guide and it can be improved.

Send me an email, let me know your thoughts. What do you think needs to be improved in these 10 steps? How do we build together? What's an example that you can provide with respect to a project, a process, an organization where you would custom design your 10 steps? I'd love to hear from you. I'd love to learn together. I hope this has served you, my 10 Essential Steps to Collaboration, my book Break Through to Yes: Unlocking the Possible Within a Culture of Collaboration because I believe collaboration is a culture. I believe that many possibilities are left unseen, untapped, unclaimed. Together we are better. Together we can do a far better job. So, let's get out there and collaborate. I look forward to hearing from you. I hope this has served you. Thank you.

Chapter 3 Great Leaders Know That They Don't Know

David: Good leaders know that they don't know it all. That's what we're going to talk about today on this 15-minute podcast. We're going to talk about good leaders don't know everything. They know that they don't know it all. Curiosity is probably the most valuable qualities of a great leader. Curiosity brings us in, respects our knowledge and our perspectives and allows us to engage, allows the leader to be smarter, more engaged, have their people respect them as well. It works both ways. We live in a very complex world, increasingly complex world. Collaboration is the way to get through complexity. No one leader can get through it all, understand it all.

I've got a long-term business partner, Bruce McIntyre. He and I met in 1996 and he invited me to join his company, a little natural gas exploration company. And we worked together in five companies between 1996 and 2007. One diamond mining exploration company and the rest were a little oil and gas exploration companies in Canada. When I asked Bruce for his advice on collaboration and leadership because I've got a tremendous respect for Bruce McIntyre. He has a ton of integrity, a great leader, he's very collaborative and probably like you, really likes to have a small group, very wise people that will challenge him, inform him, keep him in right direction.

For my book, Break Through to Yes, I asked Bruce; "When isn't collaboration appropriate? "Bruce gave me – this aren't his exact words but this is his message. Bruce McIntyre said, "Collaboration isn't useful in about 1% of the time of a president, 1%. And that's the time when you must get things fixed. So, if somebody is out of alignment, their interests are different, their performance is poor. That's when you need to step up and have them step out.

Otherwise, 99% of his time is focused on working together better and I really respect that."

Another man I think is a great collaborator, another friend of mine in Calgary over to Canada is Jim McCormick. Jim was the past president of the Progressive Conservative Association of Alberta for at least a decade. The conservative has gone through power and failure. Jim gave me another quote. In my book, Break Through to Yes, I have a hundred people from five countries quoted, a hundred people from five countries. They are the ones that have the wisdom. I believe I'm in integrity by having a book on collaboration that's actually a collaborative book. So, Jim told me, "The capacity of a leader to provide a direction, to leave that dream of what can be requires successful inclusion of and continual engagement of all stakeholder groups." That's leadership. Capacity of a leader to provide a direction, to weave that dream of what can be requires successful inclusion and engagement constantly of all stakeholders.

So how do we do this if curiosity is the way to learn together, to find out things together? I'm thinking about math right now and often people will say, "Well, with collaboration, one plus one equals what?" Well again, equals 11. Yeah, two ones. Bad joke, bad metaphor but think about that. How many times in your life, in your career, your family, have you worked together and you've come to a conclusion that you had not expected and it was better than what you'd expected? I hope it's often. I hope it's more often soon. I believe that that's true. How do you listen? Well, we listen together, we listen for opportunity, we listen deeply, we engage.

As a negotiator, I often see companies and negotiators get themselves into trouble. They get themselves into trouble when they think about the deal they believe they've just made. Now, that deal could be oil and gas deal, it could be building a wind firm, it could be a solar firm. It could be a deal with an indigenous first nation. And after a long, hard and successful negotiations, stop, ask the person across the table, "What do you think we've just agreed to?" And I promise you, when you ask that question, there'll always be more. There'll be things where you'll say, "Hmm, it's mostly right but, yeah." Those buts are deadly word. Let's find out that but way earlier because if you hand off your agreement to a bunch of lawyers or contracts people or even if you go apart for a week and then get back together, there are most always be that, but. So even when you're certain, ask, be curious, be a leader. It engages others, it clarifies, and it builds the wisdom.

I want to come back now to thinking about, okay, that's a brave statement for any leader to declare, "I don't know it all." It seems pretty obvious, common sense but – but, there is that word again. But no one can know it all. Well perhaps, if I'm making handles for skipping ropes for children in Nunavut, maybe I can be an expert in handles in skipping ropes for children in Nunavut, Canada, Northern Canada, but there's not much else. I know that I don't understand my children. I know that I don't understand my wife. I certainly know that I don't understand Donald Trump or Hillary Clinton or Angela Merkel. You noticed what I did there? I went to people I love, people that I'm different with, asking questions, being curious helps me understand, helps me to know, help me to connect, helps me to be more strategic. Leaders do know that they do not know it all. So how do we find it out?

Well, earlier today I had a conversation with a collaborator about listening. How do you listen? Are you thinking about what you're going to say next? There's that story, I didn't make it up but I've used it over the years that in our city, the person that stops talking for a moment is declared the listener. That's so not true. There is so much more power in listening. You get to explore, you get to be curious, you get to learn, you get the honor and respect, you get to be in a place of innovation. Think about dispute resolution. Think about the time it takes to resolve a conflict through mediation. In the four-step model of mediation, solving the problem doesn't come until the last probably 10% of the process, the last 10%.

So, after the introductions, exploring what the issues are, what are the resources, who's involved, all of that is step one. Step two is exploring underlying interest, exploring – as we've said in another podcast, finding the truth in this subject with this group of people on this topic, today. Third stage is exploring options, and then the fourth is reaching agreement. That second step of the mediation four-stage process and the best mediation is the majority of the time, sometimes it's 60% of the time. Whether it's a morning, or a week, or a month, keep listening, keep checking, keep being curious. Go deeper, deeper, deeper. What are the motivators here? What's does that? What did it feel like? And what's the magic of that, of knowing that you don't know and being curious and checking and rechecking and rechecking and not reacting or defending or arguing? That other person feels like they've been heard when I can state back to them what their experience has been, what the feeling was, what the interests were and what the hope and aspirations were.

Two beautiful things resolved. One is, they finally feel heard. Now they can let you speak. They finally feel heard. And secondly, once they're heard, they're ready to reach agreement, to figure it out together. It is very, very critical. Now there are times with family, with my wife – well, I'm not very good at that. I want to declare my way and I'm smart. They're wrong, I'm right. How often do you think that works? Think about your relationships, how often does that work when you tell your partner, your father, your boss, your child, your leaders you've got it all figured out, they're wrong and they just better figure stepping line with you. It rarely works, rarely works for any of them either. So, let's come together, let's collaborate, let's explore together, let's listen together. Where are we?

That brings me to another sense of listening and curiosity, our primary qualities of collaboration and leadership, agreement building. Doing is less than important than intentions. Step one, set intention in my Break Through to Yes book, my ten essential steps. Doing and getting in the way, we can do far less if we focus on our relationship and the quality, quality of our relationships. And in fact, number of years ago, I designed a new to-do list, you know those lists that you've got on your desk or on your fridge? Here's the five things I need to do today. I switched that for my clients. I gave out To-do lists which are To-be lists.

Here is my To Be list. Part one, what is my intention right now. So, we can do it once a day or before a meeting. Part two, how do I consciously choose to be today, integrity, honesty, curiosity, listening deep, creative, fun. Anything that you want to be, write it down, be conscious, choose that. And then, once you've got from the intention to how you choose to show up today what you choose to be in this moment, then you can write no more than three to-dos. Anything more than three things to do in a day, you're really not doing the most important things. Write down the three most important things and everything else is just business.

I refer to my friend and business partner and former boss, Bruce McIntyre earlier in this podcast. He said something amazing to me a long time ago. He said, "David, our shareholders pay us and they pay us well not to be busy and work 70 hours a week. They pay us to come up with one brilliant innovation each year and to capture it, to turn that into value, to turn that into profits, to turn that into success." Just one. That's all. One idea can triple your share price so don't value the business, value the relationship, the innovation, the qualities that you show up in. Today's podcast, we really talked about curiosity as a primary value to leaders because the great leaders know that they do not know it all.

Chapter 4 Global Book Release Celebration

David: Hello. This is David B. Savage. Today, March 22nd marks the worldwide release of my book, Break Through to Yes: Unlocking the Possible Within a Culture of Collaboration. This is a huge day for me and thank you for joining me on this podcast.

A couple of weeks ago, a publicist from Boston called me up and said, "David, your book could not be more timely. It is so needed right now." In American politics, it's so divisive, so unintelligent, so separate whether it's democrats or republicans. I would add to that, climate change, Syria refugees, income disparity, social outrage. I hope part of Break Through and I hope part of our conversation is about coming together, about getting to one yes, respect, inclusion, diversity. This world is not black and white. This world is increasingly complex and yet, we've got the tools, the internet, Skype, whatever that we can contact people around the world. It used to be six degrees of separation. I believe there's only two now, maybe three in some cases, between you and the person with the information, the resources or the challenge that will serve you best.

Let me share something I'm very proud about is Kirkus. Kirkus is like the consumer reports of book. They rate books. When my editor at Elevate Publishing in Idaho said, "We should go for a Kirkus review." So, I go, "Okay, what's that all about?" And he said, "Well, they don't like many books but we should be able to get something from them, something that we can use to marketing and share this great book." Well, I was just thrilled in January when Kirkus reviews came up with this. Let me just read this for a moment with you. Break Through to Yes: Unlocking the Possible Within a Culture of Collaboration thoroughly examines the power of successful collaborations. Canadian collaboration expert, Savage offers a work that couldn't be timelier. While it addresses organizational collaboration, this book could be interpreted more broadly as a Treatise on building a cooperative culture within families, groups, businesses and government.

I am thrilled and I am timely. And you're here with me, so that means you are timely. We have this collective consciousness, this will to make our world a better place. That's why you're here, that's why I'm here. Three years ago, when I decided that, "Yeah, I'm going to write this book, step out, be seen," I looked around on working together. Because in my four-year career, it's all about building capacity, building groups, building companies, building not-for-profits, building learning. I looked at collaboration as my frame, how to work together better. I looked at bestselling books on collaboration. There wasn't many in 2012, 2013. The other thing that I noticed is none of them were actually collaborative books. All of those at the time were written by one, two or even possibly three authors.

I wanted our book to be different, I wanted our book to be collaborative and that's what we've done. In my book that comes out today, this is an inclusion of over a hundred people from five countries have included their wisdom, their challenge, their sense of what you need, what are their characteristics and what you want to avoid in collaboration, have included it all. Isn't that cool? To my book, I'm the only author. I'm the one that's on the title page, on the cover. And yet, as an example of my belief about oneness and connection and one, two or three degrees of separation, I reached out. And I think about 80% of the people I reached out to saying, "Could you give me your wisdom on collaboration?" Eight percent of them came back with their wisdom. Their responses to my questions, their own insights, they're all in the book. So, thank you to them, thank you to those additional 45 guests.

I've got a Voice America podcast program. You can pick it up on iTunes in 16 episodes, 47 guests. I hope you can see the integrity in what I'm doing. I hope that you can understand and be welcome and do it yourself. I just had a great conversation with Eric Leeman of Sandy Hook New York. His children were in Sandy Hook school that faithful day a few years ago. It's changed his life. We are finding ways to support each other. We may in fact meet and do something together, a TED talk or a workshop or simply meet and exchange and include others in Paris this coming May.

I credit my friend Richard Schultz for making that introduction. The theme here is let's get together, let's reach out beyond the mediates, beyond the media, the politicians, those that want to divide and make us more ignorant through triggering our amygdala, our reptilian brain. Celebrate your network. Expand your network. We must work together far better. In my book, I offer 100 people plus 47 people and 10 essential steps. Like negotiation, dispute resolution in leadership, collaboration is its own field of study and works well when consciously collaborate. Consciously collaborate, just think about that for a moment. What is my intention? How do I design this? What's the vision? Those are the things in my book.

A great mentor of mine, friend of mine and somebody I think is a world leader in leadership and dispute resolution, Ken Cloke. He was on my Voice America podcast and he said something that I just want to share with you now. "It doesn't matter whose end of the boat is sinking, we're all in this together. We must realize that we must take responsibility for it and start working on our problems together. It doesn't mean it's easy. It just means it's the truth." Ken also shared with me that there are many scales of collaboration, small scale, big scale, global scale. And when we start to see each other, when we start to work together consciously and with the intention of building a shared future that we all desire, I think it is much easier.

So, my point is, start with respect, what is your honest intention. Collaboration isn't a meeting. When do you collaborate? When don't you collaborate? There's a crossover here about leadership. What is leadership in collaboration? Some leaders use collaboration as a way of avoiding leadership and authority and responsibility and accountability and vision. Well, let's have a meeting. That's not collaboration. That's avoidance. Collaboration to me is a culture and that's why I named my book, a culture of collaboration, how we are together, how we serve together, how we work together.

It's a big hope, it's a big dream, it's my invitation to all of us to Break Through to yes. I see this as an important step. I would like to hear from you, email me. We can circumvent those that want to divide us. We can find better ways to work together. It could be working on a – well, any number. I've got a whole list but they're not your list. Share what you need help on. We can create a global map of resources of people resources, funding, intelligence that would serve your projects and would serve your organization. We can do that now.

So, I hope you buy my book. More importantly, I hope you gain your wisdom. And if we can have an opportunity to have a conversation where we can support each other, that is my hope. My hope is that the next generation does it far better, find solutions, finds community, protect the environment, builds business. My call to action is be open. What might three other perspectives be? How might you find your truth? Send me an email on your perspectives on collaboration.

It is so misunderstood and we're at a point where it is so important. Wars, climate change, income disparity, outrage, judgment, these can be reduced. No, I'm not foolish enough to say that they can be eliminated, no. Sometimes they're necessary but they can be reduced. Just going back to another statement that my friend Ken Cloke shared with me is, the first thing that's misleading is that there is a single thing that is known as collaboration. We can certainly think of it as singular but we can also think of it as having a kind of infinite manifestations. Yeah, infinite and yours. If I can recommend a great book, another great book, The Dance of Opposites by Ken Cloke. Check that out.

So, what have we learned today? Step in to your power, collaborate, access the resources, people, the funding, the network. Perhaps one of the things that we could do together is map that network based on your intention, where are the resources that are serving you. It may not be in your village, or your city, or your school or your company. Probably isn't. We tend to stay on those silos way too long. There's no need for it. This is the time where we can access.

A friend talked about disruptive technology to me. Well, I'm hopeful that our collaborations will disrupt. I'm hopeful that we find new pathways, we can create a new economy. In my podcast series, we're going to talk about shared value. So that's designing projects that serve business, community and the environment, designing them early together. And again, we must work together for our better. Check out the book. Think of collaboration as its own field of study and how you will do it. Yes, I give you 10 essential steps, I give you 100 plus points of wisdom. Mostly, I want to build our community. Like Eric, he in New York, concerned about violence, concerned about videogame violence. Guess what, my son is a videogame developer in Los Angeles. They are now connected. They are having a conversation about the evolution of video gaming.

What's next? What's healthy? What creates what we want, the future we want? It's so simple, so easy. So, in closing, thanks so much for listening to me for this fifteen minutes. Whenever you have a judgment, whenever you see a certainty broadcast from anyone, ask yourself, "What are the three other perspectives that I'm not hearing here?" Ask yourself that. Hope you enjoy the book. I'm delighted today. This was a book that when I wrote it, it was three years of hard work, majority of my time, lots of resources. I hope it matters. It matters to me. I hope it matters to you. I hope it's like a handbook that you'll refer to a number of times. Let's Break Through to yes and unlock those possibilities that are just waiting for us. Thanks.

Chapter 5 EGOS

David: What is the key reason collaboration fails? What's the big barrier to working together for high performance? Let me just ask that again. What do you think the big barrier is? Well, that's today's topic. I'm David B. Savage, author of Break Through to Yes. My answer to the big barrier, the key reason collaboration fails is the topic for today, ego, ego, ego, ego. We're tricked by our ego or giving up control to other rock stars, folk that simply want to take control and take charge, take our power. When you get a moment if you've bought my book, Break Through to Yes: Unlocking the Possible Within a Culture of Collaboration or if you haven't, look at it on my website or on Amazon, Barnes & Noble, Chapters, wherever it's easy for you. Check out that cover because we designed it to be clean, simple and have some aspects there where – while it's clean and simple, you want to look twice. There's more to it than initially you see. It's kind of like collaboration.

What I'm suggesting that you do is take a look at that cover. There are four letters that have shading behind them. I looked and looked and looked thinking how can I make my book cover more interesting. Is there an acronym behind all those letters in the title? I couldn't find it. My publisher Elevate couldn't find it. One morning in Calgary, I was having breakfast with Donna Hastings, the chief executive officer of the Heart and Stroke Foundation of Alberta, Nunavut and the Northwest territories. I asked her if she could see something that would be an acronym that would be on message for my book cover. She looked at it, she looked at it and guess what she saw that I hadn't seen, E-G-O-S. In Break Through to Yes, you'll see E-G-O-S shaded. That's kind of cool and it is the double meeting, that second look to say, "Oh, egos are the shadiness of collaboration." Those leaders, those participants, they've already made up their mind, they've got the solution, they know it right and they discount the process and the people and the other perspectives, egos.

Ego is not manipulation. Ego should be a service to our world, to our community and to our companies, to ourselves, to our families. That's what leaders do, they build those up, egos. When we look at rock star leaders, we set ourselves apart from the system, our own development, our commitment and we set them up to fail as well. We build them up to knock them down. In America, couple recent examples are President Barack Obama. So much hope, so much frustration after eight years. He's just a man in a system. He didn't have the power that most of us believe the presidents of the United States have. Donald Trump, so popular and his own party is working hard to defeat him.

One of my favorite fiction authors is Stephen King. And on Twitter, one of the things that Stephen King said just few weeks ago was a little interesting. "The Tea Party of the Republican Party has worked so hard to build somebody just like Donald Trump. And now that they have him, they're not very happy. They're fearing that Donald Trump or his like will never allow the republicans ever to be president again." So, whether it's Donald Trump or Barack Obama or Justin Trudeau or whomever, they're just people. Let's stop looking to those huge egos, those big people.

A good friend of mine has edited probably a dozen best-selling books. She lives in Upstate New York. And in 2012 when I was looking at writing, thinking about editing, thinking about a publicist and a publisher and how do I create Break Through to Yes, she told me, "David, I like you but I must be honest with you. The publishing industry today wants to see you as a rock star with a secret sauce that you've developed out in the hinter lands of Canada and that publisher is going to bring the secret sauce and you to the world to save us." Well, that's a sad statement and I

38

believe her. That's often what we do in politics, entertainment, leadership in organizations. We get the rock stars and we set them up to fail. We do. It's hard on them. Let's manage our expectations. Let's raise the expectations for us to work together.

We can be frustrated with lack of progress by our politicians or by our corporate leaders, and they are simply part of the system. The sooner they realize that, that they need to align the system, work together better, negotiate, collaborate, resolve conflicts, include and invite and dream together the faster we're going to get to where our yes is.

I have an organization called The Collaborative Global Initiative that Duncan Autrey and I formed probably two and a half, almost three years ago now, focusing on collaborative leadership, conflict management, stakeholder engagement, shared value, visioning. Around North America and around the world. Kathy Porter is one of our members. Cathy shared with me, there's a synergy that comes from a well-functioning group that is very powerful. I often use that example from the movie of many years ago, Apollo 13? Do you remember that, Apollo 13?

When they were stuck up there, they had to get these guys in a room and said, "Here's what you've got, figure it out." They had to work together to find a solution and they did. It's a great movie, great example of no matter what the threat, there are consequences. We can figure it out. Apollo 13 did get back to earth. They innovated together. There was no time for egos in that one.

So, my point in this podcast is that we are better when we work together. We are better when we include, innovate and share collective wisdom. It's really bad math, but I believe 1 + 1 can equal 11. I know that when I collaborate successfully, the outcome is always more brilliant than I'd even dreamed. How are you in your organization? What's your role? What's your hope?

What's your frustration? Do you choose to be a messenger, a doer, a challenger, a leader? What's your choice?

Sometimes I'll just be a messenger, sometimes I'll make the coffee and sometimes I will be very disruptive, I will challenge, I will stand up, I will fight for what I believe. That's part of my book, Break Through to Yes. We encourage people, encourage you to stand up for your values. There is no reason on earth that you separate your values and your dreams. Bring something else to work, it's like a work coat that you put on. Okay, this isn't really me but this is what the boss, and these shareholders and my peers want me to be. That doesn't work, that creates stress, misalignment, wasted opportunities.

A leader is most successful when she or he focuses on the whole, not on their power, not on their compensation, their legacy. They're more successful when they do it together. It's the only way. A woman I have a great regard for is Margaret Wigley. Her quote and I'll read this one, "When leaders take back power, when they act as heroes and saviors they end up exhausted, overwhelmed and deeply stressed. So, the hero, the rock star taking the power from us. We can't allow them to be overwhelmed, we need to support them and they need to support us." So, what do we see?

It takes time to change the culture from command and control where power is isolated and shift it to collaboration. I'm a visual per and I think of – I enjoy road biking, I enjoy being on my mountain bike. Road biking is something I took up about three years ago, do it poorly, slowly but I do it. I'm out there on the road. I've ridden in three Gran Fondos and had a lot of fun.

Think of collaboration as the peloton in road bike racing. Road bike racing, think of the Tour de France. In a peloton, in road bike racing like Tour de France, what I realized is, the group pulls me along. Literally, if I can tuck in to that back of that group often when they're passing me, if I tuck in, they're slipstreaming, we're slipstreaming, we're all faster together. Literally, you could feel it in that peloton on the side of a road. It is fantastic. And in the peloton, notice that when a person doesn't stay at the front of that peloton for more than minutes, maybe ten minutes, but that's where they overwhelm. The stress, the exhaustion comes if you're trying to break the wind for everybody else, you rotate.

Think of yourself in your organization, your family, your nation as a peloton. Don't give away your power. Don't ignore your own wisdom. Don't be afraid. Step in. Vision what you choose and create it together. I'd love to hear how this is working for you, what's your thoughts are. What is the project or a skill that you like to develop further? How might I help you to connect you to that network, connect you, challenge you, include you? Look for ways to share power. And if I can say anything, my call to action this week, learn from people that are not in agreement with you and (b) open to unexpected outcomes.

When organizations come to me, in the last seven months I've started to ask presidents in organization that want to hire me a key question, "How comfortable are you not knowing the outcome of this initiative?" The reason I ask that, you can probably guess. Because if that leader already has a pre-determined outcome and wants the group to just make it happen, that's not collaboration, that's project management. Collaboration means openness to unexpected outcomes. And in my life, in my work, when I've been open to other's voices, experiences, potentials, dreams, the outcome is most always been grander then what I expected. Lead from there. I hope you've enjoyed this 15 minutes together. I sure have. Look forward to a conversation with you. Take good care.

Chapter 6 How Collaborative is my organization?

David: How collaborative is my organization? That's the topic for today's podcast. How collaborative is my organization? What gets measured gets done. Yeah, I believe that. We need a way to assess how collaborative your organization is, my organization, others and where improvements maybe positively transformative. I've been a business person since 1975. I've worked in command and control top down organizations, but really, since 1993, I've only worked for myself. I've either founded the company, co-founded the company. And the beauty of that is to be able to select the people that you work with. Trust, complementary skills, ability to be honest with each other and having a similar dream are really important.

I'm David Savage. My book is Break Through to Yes: Unlocking Possibility Within a Culture of Collaboration. Check it out. Let's tune up your team. When I talk about my 41 years, companies like Ashland Oil and Total Petroleum. In American and French oil gas companies in Canada, I was just a cog in the wheel. And then starting with Westar Petroleum, BXL Energy, Collaborative Global Initiative, Kootenay Leadership, I was one of few smaller organization with 230 people. That's much easier, but it's important to actually be honest together, to be able to challenge each other, not be comfortable. And trust each other not to be stepping on each other's toes, collaborating not competing with each other, keeping your egos away as we've talked about previously.

In my belief in the assessments I've done on leadership and teams, whether its nine domains, whether it's my own work, whether it's the leadership circle, others, companies that do the assessments are often disappointed that they're not as great as they thought they were. This insight through an assessment really helps people to measure where they are, what needs to be celebrated and what needs to be improved. That's right. So, one of the things that I've put on my website is a collaboration assessment app. There are series of questions that helps us understand how collaborative your organization is, where are the gaps, where are the strengths. The reason I did that is often assessment is a good entry point to a conversation and it's a good process, a good system to continuously gauge, measure, develop, improve and celebrate.

So, there is damage done when organizations are not collaborative. Dysfunctional leaders in organizations disconnected people, reduce the opportunities, reduce the impact, buy in, destructive. All sorts of reasons that command and control, rock star hero CEOs can really disconnect and people don't give their all. They show up, do what they're told, they don't innovate, they don't challenge, they don't stand up, they don't debate. And many leaders and teams like I said are not as good as they think they are. There is an opportunity for continuous learning. Your work is not just a job.

So, go to my assessment tool on my website www.davidbsavage.com. Along with SVI of Dallas, I offer you the world's first Collaborative Leadership and Team Development 360 Assessment on my website.

For a simpler introduction, go to page 61 on my book, Break Through to Yes: Unlocking Possibility Within a Culture of Collaboration. This is an assessment tool that is deep and it's preliminary. It's a good starting place. I credit Laura Hummelle of Ahead of the Curve Consulting and Kathy Porter of the Collaborative Global Initiative for helping me develop this assessment. My hope is we will continue to develop it. Once the assessment is done, you'll get a report, you'll get some feedback and there'll be an opportunity to work together on improving your collaborative culture and your outcomes, your profits.

In the assessment tool, there are principles like inclusion, transparency, embracing conflict, embracing diversity. Mostly, having one another's back. Yeah, the Attachment Theory. Whether it's in your family or in your corporation or your community, when you have one another's back, it's a safe place to be more courageous. So, let's look at some of the questions on the assessment tool. Add your own if you like. We'd love to hear from you. We can build this assessment and we can build your understanding, build my understanding by working together on it.

But here are some questions. On a scale of 1-5, how well do we listen to each other in our organization? Scale of 1-5; 5 being all the time constant, we can paraphrase, we felt heard; 1 would be, no, we're thinking about what we're thinking about and thinking about what we're going to say, we're not really listening to each other. Another question was, how are we held accountable for our duties, our roles, our responsibilities? Are those accountabilities clear, transparent? Are we held accountable? Or when we miss, when we screw up, when we fail, is it just ignored because we want to be nice with each other? Are we beat up for failure? How are we held accountable to one another and how is that experienced by everybody in the team? Scale of one to five.

We're anxious to share our failures and experiences and open it up for discussion on how to do it better next time. That'd probably be a four or a five. Sometimes when we think about giving a 1 or 2 of 5, it's uncomfortable. We don't want to embarrass somebody. We'll punish them later. If a leader does that then they are, probably, a 1 out of 5.

Another question is, we have established teamwork principles, here's how we work together, here's our rules of engagement. What would be a five in our teamwork principles? They're written down, they're simple, they're short, they're understandable, they're embraced by all.

When I ask that question, what are your teamwork principles; you'd be able to answer me in one sentence quickly, that would be a five. That's not common. A one would be principles, principles, we don't need principles. We just need to get the job done. That would be a one because nobody knows the rules.

How do our work on principles when we work together? How do they align with our values? What are the values that all of us stand for in this corporation, organization, entity? What are they? Values and ethics are the foundation of great leadership. Well, I guess they're the foundation of poor leadership too, it just depends on whether you agree or not. Are they published? Do you agree with them? Are there values that you think should be there that aren't there? Another question on the assessment is, we seek out those that speak out. In other words, do we make sure that the system embraces conflict? Do we make sure that the system, the people, the leaders, the round tables, the projects and initiatives really look for constructive critiques? It's so key. Without a critic, we have group think, we have a bunch of "yes people" and we may drive right off a cliff a together. What are the systems, the ways that we can evidence that we value those that disagree?

About 2008, I was in Upstate New York at a Nine Domains training. This great training went on for about three weeks. Beautiful work through the Enneagram. The Enneagram is something I highly recommend. Nine Domains is for teams, levels of functioning for teams. And throughout the three weeks, the group was very much together, "Yeah, this is great, this is great." And I kept sitting back and thinking, "There's something wrong here, something just doesn't fit for me." I'm not quite sure how to explain it and I tried to explain it a number of times over the time we were there. And finally, the second last day, I said it in words that they could hear and that I could hear that was clear to me. As I spoke up -- I spoke out and said,

"No, this doesn't and here's why. This is what's missing for me."

And it that room, about 50 people turn towards me and said, "You're right. David, you're right. We missed that. That's important. So glad you raised it." That was a healthy team. Some teams, we've both been involved in, we're going to push it under the water or under the rug, push me under the water, who knows, just to get it done. It's not perfect but this is the best we have. Well, let's make it better. Let's speak out when there's something different. So, think about going through, filling out the collaborative assessment. See how collaborative your culture is, your organization is, where are the gaps. I'll give you a report. I'll give you a feedback. We can build on that conversation and learn together.

I like to advance that assessment because I think it's important to have a tool such as this. I think it's very important. What gets measured gets done. What gets measured gets improved. And most importantly, the assessment can then be taken to your team, to your family, to your community, to your political party to custom design it. Yeah, this is good work. Complete the assessment, start the conversation, design your new high-performance organization or team starting now. That's my call to action for you today. Step in to your Yes, relook, rethink your organization and team, use the tools that are available to become more successful through collaborative culture, through embracing conflict, embracing accountability, embracing diversity. Step in and step up. Thanks so much for listening to me today. I hope some of these made sense to you. I hope I hear from you and we can help tune up your team, you can help tune up my assessment and my work. Let's collaborate. Thanks again. This is David B. Savage, Break Through to Yes: Unlocking the Possible Within a Culture of Collaboration.

48

Chapter 7 Collaboration is the Way; Shared Value is the Destination

David: Collaboration is the way. Shared value is the destination. Welcome. Today in our 15-minute podcast, I want to talk about shared value and how to get there. In this world of conflicting interest, challenging people, stressed communities and increasingly over challenged environment, businesses can Break Through to yes. We do this through shared value. What are we going to talk about today? We're going to explain shared value. We're going to talk about collaboration and we're going to give you some opportunities to create great things in service of your company, your community and our planet.

Welcome. This is David B. Savage. My book is Break Through to Yes: Unlocking the Possible Within a Culture of Collaboration. So why change, why do things different? Well, projects just don't move forward. Communities get separated and block projects. People are divided on many issues. You think of the American presidential campaign right now, how divisive that is. Even the Republican Party turning on itself. Wow. Shared value means turning that to the good, to the positive where whatever we do as business people, we create and obtain and earn our shared value because of shared value. We create profits for our shareholders by placing the community on equal standing with the economy and equal standing on the environment.

The "me first" attitude, the command and control, "I don't really care what everybody else is doing, this is what I'm doing" attitude just doesn't work anymore. We got to look for bigger outcomes. Cumulative effects are real. Often our projects are deemed acceptable or not acceptable or conditionally acceptable based on their merits alone. In some occasions, regulatory bodies look at cumulative effects. That means if my project is the 10th wind farm in Minnesota, I need to look at the cumulative effect of all the prior nine plus my tenth. It, also, means maybe my 10th wind farm in Minnesota is the most attractive, the most inventive, the most best priced, least in the way of another people's interest. We must look at the whole picture. Our industry, our nation, our world is increasingly complex, and we must look at the whole. We can't continue to fragment and go by hero, command and control, self-centered leaders.

Recently, at the Haskayne School Business at the University of Calgary; Daniel Clarke, President of CSV Midstream; David Milia of the University of Calgary and I presented a talk entitled Collaboration is the Way; Shared Value is the Destination. So why am I talking to you today, is to bring the whole, the completeness through collaboration. What is shared value? Well, it means more than providing social good or investing or caring and externally driven responsibility to do so. It is achieving greater impact to ensure the communities we work in and around those communities will grow alongside us. CSV or Creating Shared Value demonstrated social and environmental improvement with a connection to economic value creation for the company and the community.

Earned value is not just shared or distributed. It is created by increasing capacity and providing the tools to empower the communities to succeed. We are all in this together. I know you understand this and it's complex. It is challenging. Creating shared value takes great leadership. And how on earth do you think we can create shared value for communities, the environment and companies? By doing it by ourselves? We can't. We must collaborate. We must come through together. How do we do this? Well, let me talk a little bit more about the pain.

The pain here includes the ideas in the 2016 World Economic Forum. Google 2016 World Economic Forum. And what they highlight is the highest risk, and the highest cost and the highest impact to our global economy today, this year. It's scary. Water shortage, clean water availability, food, climate change, energy price collapse, cybercrime, increasing income disparity. Let's be part of the solution to these things or any one of them. In our way, think local. In our way, in our organizations, our families, our communities, let's start to collaborate. So how do we do that? Well I think it's simple. I've got a whole book full of advice, Break Through to Yes: Unlocking the Possible Within a Culture of Collaboration.

And in this mindset, the culture is global culture. The culture is self-culture. Start by looking at your values, what are your values, what are the things that you lead from, your foundations for how you are in this world. Connect with others, talk to them about their values. Create a list of what values you share. Then think about, consider, develop a shared vision of the future for your family, for your company, for your community. What does that look like? As a coach, I find that's the way to get people unstuck most often, is go to the future state, the preferred state. What do we want to create together?

So, once you've got your shared values identified, once you've dreamed your shared future, then look to create shared value. So shared values, vision, shared value. The way to do this is by collaboration. It must be this way. It can't be any other way. It can't be dictated. We can't be run by Donald Trumps or Hillary Clintons, Angela Merkel. It comes from us. When we collaborate, we can create new innovative business models and projects that are win-win. We will do this. If you like music and if you want to give yourself four minutes of a smile, go to chuckrose.ca and listen Win or Walk Away. It's a song that my friend Chuck wrote, performed and recorded and gave me permission to play and have you access. It's not good enough the old way. We need to serve our shared values.

So, if the World Economic Forum sees those threats and many, many more, you'll see the interconnectedness of all those threats. Let's be part of the solution. How do we do that? Well, I don't know the answers. I've got a guide book, my Break Through to Yes, I designed as a handbook that you can refer to over and over again. Even running meetings, simply running meetings, you can do this. Look at the 10 steps from a meeting-planning perspective, meeting-leader perspective. I invite you, email me, and I'll send you a template where I've taken my 10 essential steps to collaboration and address them specifically to meetings. I hope that helps you. I'll send it to you.

Remember Monty Python? Meetings, bloody meetings. Well, I think we've all experienced collaboration, bloody collaboration. Let's do it right. Let's do it together. Let's create that shared value. So, what's in it for me? Of course, self-interest is always got to be part of this. We can't always be serving people, planet and prophets, must service you as well. Well I assert, I argue and I have examples where creating shared value creates greater profits and results for me as well. I've got many examples, whether it's when I was in the oil and gas industry, running small oil and gas companies, listening deeply to the opposers, including all the voices, including everyone with an interest and then finding that there is a solution that none of us have ever dreamed of separately. We save capital cost, we are welcomed by the neighborhood, we are welcomed by area gas processing facilities. And our shared price doubled or tripled within about six months.

And other dialogue that my Collaborative Global Initiative is creating, working on is we're now working with a group in San Luis Obispo, California on the topic of the Diablo Canyon nuclear facility. Its permit expires in about eight years and there'll be regulatory process, there'll be corporate process. Pacific Gas and Electric will be doing what they can. And we're convening dialogue, conversation where all the voices get heard, all the interest get heard. We can come together and understand what are our shared values in San Luis Obispo in California, in America, in North America, in the world. How does San Luis Obispo want to look 10 years from now? How might we innovate? Instead of saying yes or no, how might we innovate? How might we collaborate and create something that's greater than any of us apart can do? We have those opportunities. We have those great opportunities.

Even on a family basis, when you listen deeply and allow others in, it changes, it balances the power. Now as a leader, you still have the ultimate power. As a CEO, a chairman, a president, you still make the final decisions and you have the accountability. As a father or a mother, same thing. But when you can collaborate with your teenagers, when you can understand and embrace and honor their interest, they fight so hard for power, allow them to be seen, allow them to be involved. The outcomes are so much better than we expect. When I'm a command and control father, I just get a lot of resistance. When I'm a collaborative father, my daughter responds far better. She gains her power and we both create the future we want.

So, in summary, collaboration is the way and shared value is the destination. I'll help you with my book, Break Through to Yes: Unlocking the Possible Within a Culture of Collaboration. I also speak to groups. I also help groups design their collaborations. I consult and I coach. There are many ways that we can work together and I know that however that is, it's inclusive and it will lead to a greater outcome, faster approval and more embraced from the world that we live in. Collaboration is the way. Shared value is the destination. Thank you. This is David B. Savage. I look forward to hearing your feedback, your innovations, your challenges, your thoughts with respect to meetings, collaborations and everything we've talked about today. Thanks.

Chapter 8 Building Your Collaborative Culture

David: In Break Through to Yes, it's all about building the culture of your organization. So, here's the topic for today, building your collaborative culture. What does that mean? How do I do that and why would I do that? Well, today we will talk about the differences also that occur when collaboration is how we get things done around here. Collaboration is not an event, it is not a tool in the toolbox, it's a relationship, it's how we lead. Welcome everyone. This is David B. Savage, author of Break Through to Yes.

Building your collaborative culture. I've had titles including director, president and chief operating officer as a business person since 1975. Over the years, I've seen too many and repeated failures costing sometimes in the billions because people are not a collaborative culture. Organizations are command and control, top down. One person at the top tells everybody else does. What a loss of intelligence? The mistakes that are often created by company leaders in organizations, when they try to force their agenda on others, people revolt. When you force your project or proposal, your idea, you get pushed back, you get resistance. Probably some law of physics in there, equal forces. When you invite possibility, when you invite people, when you invite conflict, when you listen and innovate, great things occur. But instead, many leaders, many organizations think, "Well, that's not my job. My job is just to get this thing done for my shareholders and for my ego."

Remember we talked about ego. Ego is the shaded letters on my book cover. Look. And thanks Donna Hastings. Ego also is the wall. When it's all about me, then it's not about you. That's offensive, you deserve more than that. So, when it's all about my projects, it doesn't matter. I don't take the time to be truly involved in the community and the issues and the challenges of the region that I'm involved and doing business in. And more so, not being a problems solver. Well, communities push back, environment often is damaged.

I don't know any business leaders in any industry: oil and gas, renewables, any industry that consciously says, "I want to damage the environment. I can save money by doing that." That's kind of a myth. But if you don't know the environment, if you don't know the cutthroat trout habitat, you don't really care then you don't really care. Those costs can be offloaded to others without you realizing it. You can get pushed back. So, if building a collaborative culture is important and it's not an event, we listen, we resolve, we create, we innovate. A collaborative culture means continuous learning, evolution. We address our compensation around collaborative success. What did we learn today? What went wrong? What do we need to change? What are the resources inside and outside our organization that we should access to do better from today on?

When bonuses are given out, what if some part of bonuses were made for failures, not for heroes? What if some part of bonuses were paid equally? Back at Westar Petroleum back in the 1990s, I think it was 1992, what we did is we created an incentive system that said, "Five percent of the revenue favorable to budget goes to a bonus system." So, in that issue, we also divided it up to say, "Okay. Yes, we will understand award, reward." Half of that bonus pool, whatever it is to the super performers, the ones that really made a difference, the leaders, the innovators, the challengers, the ones that cut our cost. And the other 50% of that pool, we shared equally. So as director and chief operating officer, I got exactly the same bonus as the receptionist in Kindersley, Saskatchewan. I had way different responsibilities, accountabilities, functions, roles than the receptionist did. But in many ways, she was equally as important, many, many ways. So, it's an inclusion, that's a respect. There is no class system in organizations that is useful.

I think that gives us a strategic advantage. I think that got us to places where – in that case, we were drilling, looking and improving one, two, three well drilling programs at that time. We realized by working together, by brainstorming, by innovating, by negotiating, we started drilling 20 well programs. We were able to successfully slash our cost by, I think it was like 15 to 20%. It was significant at that time. There are many ways. And of course, the receptionist in Kindersley, she saw those invoices, she had an awareness, a curiosity, she had a different perspective, she had a voice.

Some of the tools in my book, Break Through to Yes: Unlocking the Possible Within a Culture of Collaboration include the 10 Essential Steps. It, also, includes Collaborative Leadership 360 Assessment for organizations. How do you do that? We've talked about that in a podcast in this series. Go to my website and complete the assessment of your organization. Better yet, have several people at all levels in your organization complete that assessment. We'll get your report back, just to get a sense of how collaborative you are, what is your culture. If collaboration is the way we do things around here, is that true and how true is it?

Often, leaders in organizations think they're performing better than they are. In my reviews of things like leadership circle, my certification under the nine domains and other work that I've done, coaching and working with organizations on their collaborative culture. We find that their levels of functioning aren't as high as they thought and we find that there's very easy, very meaningful, very shareable processes and tools and awareness that we can bring to those organizations to elevate their level of functioning as a collaborative organization.

Now in my book, we've got 35 questions to help you assess. You can do it on your own. Take three of those questions and work it. The culture of collaboration includes, embraces, respects. And don't get me wrong, leadership is critically important. Through most of my 10 essential steps, leadership is creating the safe space for the ideas to come and it is also on step nine, it's now lead. Leadership also includes measurables, accountabilities, roles, responsibilities, duties, reporting, all of that stuff that we're still not very good at. We often look the other way. We'd rather avoid conflict than hold somebody accountable. Sometimes you'd rather keep under performers rather than challenging them, supporting them in a way that works for them or ultimately letting them go. Positively change the energy, the level of trust in your organization. Yeah, positively do that. If you wish to go deeper, let's talk about my Collaborative Leadership and Team Development 360 Assessment.

Now, this isn't only for a small companies or holistic leaders, this is for multinational, hugely billion-dollar businesses. In the book, American icon, Alan Mullaly and the fight to save Ford Motor Company, Bryce Hoffman tells such destructive dynamics is the way Ford executives met for many years until Mullaly got there. Mullaly demanded honest accountability on the focus on "we" not "me." It took the executives several weekly meetings before one executive decided he was likely to be fired anyway so he might as well tell the truth. Wow. "I'm going to be fired any way, I might as well be honest." Guess what, Allan Mullaly cheered rather than chided. Slowly, other found the courage to become a team and tell the truth. So, build your culture of collaboration, be the Alan Mullaly of your organization, be a visionary, create shared value through collaboration. And every moment, every day, every week, every report, consider ways that you can support the building of a collaborative culture in your organization.

Identify a wall that you've run into in one of your projects or one of your teams. Send me an and together, I'll help you identify the people, resources, ideas, possibilities where you might start over. Take a look at my collaborative assessment on my website and in my book. Consider reviewing that and completing that or even working with three of those questions within your team, start there. Building a collaborative culture happens over time, not immediately. But when you get your Break Throughs to Yes, it starts to accelerate. Now, let's build our new collaborative culture together. Thank you. This is David B. Savage. Now, let's collaborate.

Lead from love not fear. Lead from curiosity and courage not certainty and safety.

Break Through To Yes: The Collaborative Podcast Series
by David B. Savage

Book 1: The Foundations for Collaboration
includes eight 15-minute podcasts originally aired on the
Tenacious Living Network. The chapters are;

Finding Your Truth
10 Essential Steps to Collaboration
Great Leaders Know That They Don't Know
Global Book Release Celebration
EGOS
How Collaborative is my organization?
Collaboration is the Way; Shared Value is the Destination
Building Your Collaborative Culture
Thank you to Tenacious Living Radio for originally
producing these episodes.

Book 2: The Collaborative Guest Podcasts
offers three podcasts where David B. Savage was a guest on
Barry Wilson, Bob Acton and Duncan Autrey's podcasts.
The chapters are;

Fractal Friends Duncan Autrey,
        -talking about conflict resolution, communities,
        activists and collaboration
Mastering Leadership with Bob Acton,
        -exploring negotiation, collaboration and leadership
Collaboration and Cumulative Effects on our Land with
Barry Wilson,
        -sharing ideas on how we collaborate on the true
        cumulative effects of our construction, capital
        projects and communities.

Book 3: The 10 Essential Steps of Collaboration
provides you with 16 podcasts originally aired on Voice
America in 2015 and 2016. The chapters and guests are;

Why Collaborate
        Chuck Rose, Denise Chartrand
Collaboration Gone Bad
        Kathy Porter, Duncan Autrey
Our Global Campfire
        Jeanne McPherson, Allan Davis
Set Intention
        Patricia Morgan, Don Loney, David Gouthro
Be Aware
        Kenneth Cloke, Cheryl Cardinal, Ryan Robb
Embrace Conflict
        Esther Bleuel, Jeffrey Cohen
Seek Diversity
        Joan Goldsmith, Amy Fox
Design the Collaboration
        Richard Schultz, Laura Hummelle, Colin Campbell
Come Together
        Donna Hastings, Rob McKay, Art Korpach
Listen Deeply
        Tara Russell, Linda Matthie, Viki Winterton,
        Stephen Smith
Collaborate with Vision
        Dee Ann Turner, Doreen Liberto, Dana Meise,
        Teresa de Grosbois
Now Lead
        David Milia, Don Simmons, Bruce McIntyre, James
        Armstrong
Make It So
        Michael Hill, Johanne Lavoie, Atul Tandon, Prabha
        Sankaranarayan
Leadership and Team Awareness
        Bob Anderson
Next Generation Leaders and Our Future
        Dan Savage, Sarah Daitch, India Sherret, Kevin
Brown
Book Release Celebration
        David Milia, AnnaMarie McHargue

Book 4: Unlocking the Possible with Collaboration
provides you with 14 podcasts originally aired on Voice
America in 2017. The chapters and guests are;

Collaboration and Leadership
  Bob Acton, David Mitchell
Collaboration and Sports
  Tristen Chernove, Martin Parnell
Collaboration and Organizational Culture
  Mike Thompson, Stephen Hobbs
Collaboration, Company Dispute Resolution and
Mindfulness
  Julie Murray
Collaboration and Critical Thinking in This Age of Lies
  Doreen Liberto, Chuck Rose
Collaboration, Europe and Rotary International
  Elisabeth Delaygue Bevan, Florian Wackermann
Collaboration and Human Sexual Trafficking
  Lance Kadatz, Cliff Wiebe
Collaboration, Human Resources and Global Networks
  Amy Schabacker Dufrane, Japman Bajaj
Collaboration, The Secret Marathon and Going the Extra
Mile
  Kate McKenzie, Shawn Anderson, Martin Parnell
Collaboration, Leadership and Disruptive Technologies
  Jim Gibson
Collaboration, Negotiation and Mediation
  Jeffrey Cohen
Collaborative Global Initiative Tool Kit
  Barry Wilson, Doreen Liberto, Jeffrey Cohen
One Yes, One Thing, One Dream
  Deva Premal and Miten, Klara Fenlof, Robert
  Stewart, Sara Amos and Quinn Amos
Unlocking the Possible
  Kenneth Cloke, Duncan Autrey

I hope you enjoy the Break Through To Yes: The
Collaborative Podcast Series

Acknowledgements;

Thanks to everyone of my seventy-five guests from around the world on my 2015, 2016 and 2017 podcasts. Thank you to;

VoiceAmerica (Book 3 and 4),

Tenacious Living Radio (Book 1),

Obair, CE Analytic and Autrey (Book 2)

for originally producing these podcasts.

Thanks, also, to Vladimir Krstic and Pete Stover for audio production on the audio books.

And to Ginger Wilmot for transcribing the podcasts.

Unlock the Possible within a Culture of Collaboration

SAVAGE
MANAGEMENT Ltd.

About the Author;

David B. Savage, BA (Econ), PLand, CPCC
Collaboration, Business Development and Negotiation Specialist
Savage Management
Ltd.www.davidbsavage.com

Savage brings over 42-years expertise, experience and leadership in oil and gas, renewable energy, health care, entrepreneurship, stakeholder engagement and conflict management. Over a ten-year period, David and partners, collaborated to develop 5 companies and 4 not for profits. Since 2007, Savage Management has focused on build capacity, innovation and accountability in people and in and between organizations and communities.

David Savage works with leaders and organizations to advance their success through collaboration, negotiation and business development.

CORE COMPETENCIES:

Negotiations and Agreement Building, Business Development, Acquisitions, Management Consulting, plus Strategic Planning & Execution, Sustainability Engagement and Organizational Development, Management Leadership and Team Building, Stakeholder Engagement, Business Development, Conflict Management, Executive and Team Coaching plus 360 Leadership Assessments.

KEY CORPORATE EXPERIENCE:

➤ Savage Management, President, (founder, 1993 to present, private, consulting, oil and gas management, coaching, leadership and negotiation training, negotiation mastery circles and leader round tables, conflict resolution and collaboration assessments),

- Prior to 2007, David held executive positions with BXL Energy, Marmac Mines Ltd., Sebring Energy, TriQuest Energy, Sommer Energy, Westar Petroleum, Total Petroleum, Ashland Oil, Bank of Montreal, and CIBC.

PUBLICATIONS

2003: David's Company to Company Dispute Resolution Council published the Let's Talk Handbook.

2011: Think Sustain Ability published Sustain Magazine.

2012: Ready Aim Excel: 52 Leadership Lessons

2016: Break Through to Yes: Unlocking the Possible within a Culture of Collaboration

2017: The Collaborative Podcast Series (print, eBook and Audible) is now available. The Books, which include 75 guests from eight nations) are;

Book 1: The Foundations For Collaboration

Book 2: The Collaborative Guest Podcasts

Book 3: The 10 Essential Steps

Book 4: Unlocking the Possible

Break Through To Yes Updated and Revised edition

2018: Break Through To Yes: Generating More Value with Collaborative Negotiation.

PURPOSE

Getting the right people, in the right places, with the right systems and the right resources to collaborate, innovate and figure out challenges together is the best way. And, if that is not possible, then guiding the parties to the right people, principles, processes and systems to ensure everyone's interests are heard and considered is my goal.

www.ingramcontent.com/pod-product-compliance
Lightning Source LLC
Chambersburg PA
CBHW060646210326
41520CB00010B/1766